CCSS **Genre** Expository

Essential Question
What are the positive and negative effects
Wof new technology?

What About
ROBOTS?

BY YVONNE MORRIN

(bkgd) Chris Knapton/Digital Vision/Getty Images, (l) Stockdisc/PunchStock/Getty Images

We use technology every day. Machines wash our clothes and keep our food fresh. Other machines transport us, help us communicate, and entertain us. Our lives would be very different without technology!

Technology is advancing all the time. Some people are excited about these changes. Others are worried about them. Can you think of some positive effects of new technology? What are some negative effects?

Ryan McVay/Photodisc/Getty Images

Robotics is an area of technology that is developing quickly. There are millions of robots in the world. Most do jobs that are considered too dangerous or too boring for humans. Many people think robots are useful. Others believe that people might become too dependent on robots. Maybe robots will take their jobs.

Before forming an opinion about robots, look at the facts. Then you can make thoughtful conclusions. Knowing the facts also allows you to cite evidence that backs up your reasoning.

Technology affects our lives.

The word *robot* comes from a Czech word, *robota*, which means "forced labor."

One definition of a robot is that it is a machine that operates automatically in place of a human to complete a task. However, this definition fits a washing machine. A washing machine operates in place of a human so that washing clothes doesn't have to be done by hand. Yet most people would not consider a washing machine to be a robot.

Robots come in many shapes and sizes.

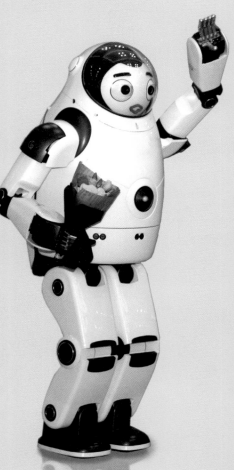

YONHAP/epa/CORBIS

(bkgd) Chris Knapton/Digital Vision/Getty Images, (t) Stockdisc/PunchStock/Getty Images

A better definition is that a robot is a machine that uses information around it to decide what to do.

A robot interacts with its environment. It uses equipment, such as cameras or microphones, to get information. A computer in the robot uses this information to make decisions. Then the mechanical parts of the robot pick up and move objects.

Between 1700 and 1900, **automatons** were invented. They were supposed to look like people or animals and they had moving parts. Some automatons could play musical instruments and draw pictures. However, automatons do not use information about their environments. They are not considered true robots.

The first machine able to make decisions was built in 1911. It played chess against humans. Electrical **sensors** told it where the chess pieces were. It moved a mechanical arm to take its turn.

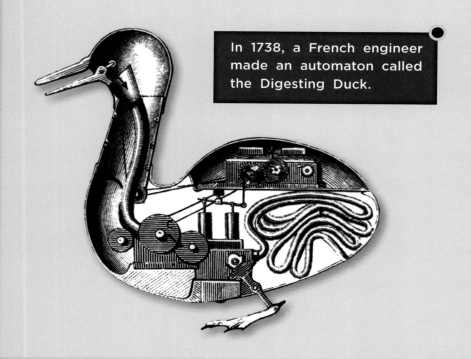

In 1738, a French engineer made an automaton called the Digesting Duck.

Photos 12/Alamy

FICTIONAL ROBOTS

Before real robots were invented, science fiction stories included robots. Some movies in the 1920s and 1930s showed robots plotting to take over Earth! In the 1950s and 1960s, robots on television were often shown as helpful companions.

In the mid-twentieth century, computer technology improved. This meant that machines could be controlled by **artificial** brains. These were the first true robots.

The first machine that could move freely and interact with its environment was made in the 1940s. As it moved, it could avoid objects. It moved so slowly that it was called Elsie the Tortoise.

STOP AND CHECK

Why aren't automatons considered to be true robots?

CHAPTER 2

Robots at Work

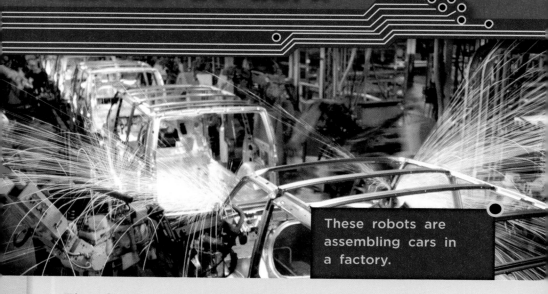

These robots are assembling cars in a factory.

The first robot designed to work in a factory had a heavy lifting arm controlled by **electronics**. In 1961, the robot was used in a factory that built cars. It lifted metal parts that were too hot for humans to handle.

In the 1960s and 1970s, robots were used in many American factories. Robots are expensive, but they can save a company a lot of money over time. That's because they:

- can often do jobs faster and more accurately than a human can;

- don't get tired and make mistakes;

- don't get bored of doing the same task over and over.

Glow Images

Robots changed factory work. Some people worried that robots would take people's jobs. They also worried about safety. Some robots that were incorrectly programmed smashed windows in a factory.

By the 1980s, most robots were **manufactured** in Japan and Europe. Japan has an aging population. People were worried that there would not be enough young workers in the future. They thought robots would be needed to do many jobs.

INDUSTRIAL ROBOT LOCATIONS

Asia leads the world in robot use.

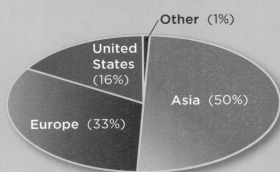

Other (1%)

United States (16%)

Asia (50%)

Europe (33%)

**VIEWPOINTS
ROBOTS IN THE WORKPLACE**

"I think having robots at work is a good idea. They can do the dangerous jobs."

"If we start using robots instead of humans at work, will I be replaced by a machine?"

What do you think? Is it a good idea to have robots in the workplace?

Too Dangerous for Humans!

Robots can be used for dangerous jobs. They can clean up chemical spills and poisonous waste in nuclear plants. Robots can even **defuse** bombs.

Robots can be used in disasters, such as earthquakes. Rescuers who search for survivors put their own lives at risk. That's why robotic scouts were developed. They carry out searches and make rescuing survivors safer.

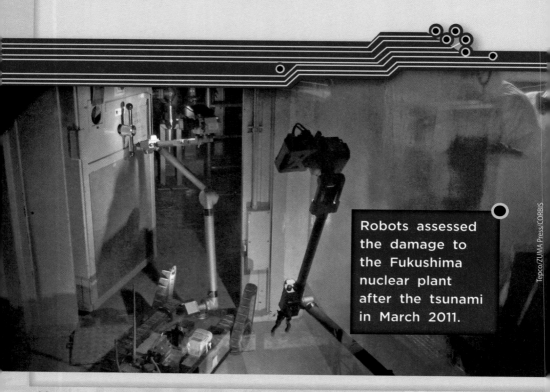

Robots assessed the damage to the Fukushima nuclear plant after the tsunami in March 2011.

Tepco/ZUMA Press/CORBIS

Robotic scouts can access dangerous areas. They carry cameras and gas detectors. These help send important information to the rescuers. These data help the rescuers to do an analysis of the situation. Robots can carry food or medicine to survivors who are trapped. Some robots can drag survivors out of the wreckage.

Engineers have developed a robotic astronaut. This robot can explore a planet's surface and pick up samples. Unlike a human, the robot doesn't need to breathe, eat, or keep warm.

STOP AND CHECK

How can robots save a company money?

This robotic astronaut is attached to a four-wheel vehicle.

Even if a human doctor is miles away, he or she can still check on patients by using a robot.

As technology advances, new uses are being found for robots.

Robots in Hospitals

Many hospitals use robots. Some robots deliver food. Others dispense medicine. Robots reduce the risk of spreading disease. They also free up nurses to do other jobs.

However, there are drawbacks to using robots in hospitals. Some people are frightened of robots. Others think that robots could make errors. Many patients prefer to interact with another human instead of a machine.

InTouch Health

SURGICAL ROBOT OPERATIONS

The number of operations performed by one popular brand of surgical robot is increasing.

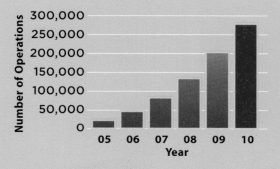

Surgical robots have been used for complex operations. Human surgeons control these surgical robots. A surgical robot is more precise than a human surgeon. Also, a robot can make a smaller cut in a patient. This means patients have less pain and heal faster.

VIEWPOINTS
ROBOTIC NURSING ASSISTANTS

Many elderly Japanese live in nursing homes. Some of them like the idea of robotic nursing assistants, but others don't.

"I don't like having a robot deliver my pills. I don't trust the robot to get it right."

"It's good that the robots bring my meals. It means nurses can spend more time with the people who need attention."

What do you think? Would you like a robot as your nurse?

"Robots might be able to solve almost all of our environmental problems. We should develop new robots to clean up the environment."

"Until we can produce robots in a more environmentally friendly way, we shouldn't make more. Spend money on preventing environmental problems first."

What do you think? Are robots good or bad for the environment?

Friend of the Environment?

Many people are not sure that the increasing use of robots is a good thing. They say that robots are made from materials that are mined. Mining can damage the environment.

These people also argue that factories that make robots use up **resources**, such as fuel and water. Throwing away outdated parts from robots can also harm the environment.

Computers contain poisonous chemicals. These chemicals can be harmful to the environment.

This robot cleans up oil that is harmful to marine life.

The counterpoint is that robots can be very helpful to the environment. Some robots can check the health of the environment and clean up **pollutants**. Some use a power source, such as solar panels, which collect energy from the sun.

Robots could help improve the environment. Some robots can sort plastic for recycling. Others can plant trees or filter pollution out of the air.

Learning from Animals

What is intelligence? Some people think intelligence means being good at analyzing data. Others believe intelligence means being able to make decisions in response to the environment.

Many engineers get robot design ideas from animals. One example is a rat-robot. The rat-robot has touch sensors in its whiskers, cameras in its eye sockets, and microphones in its ears. It can operate in the dark and be used in smoke-filled rooms or underground. Some robots have many legs so that they can walk over rough ground the way a spider does.

The rat-robot can fit into places humans can't easily go.

PIERRE VERDY/AFP/Getty Images/Newscom

STOP AND CHECK

What are three different uses for robots?

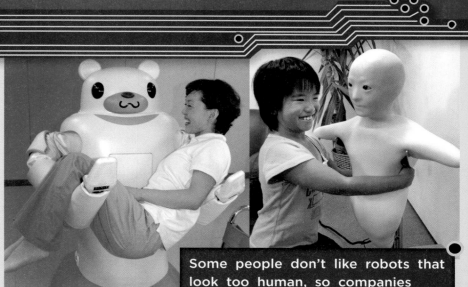

Some people don't like robots that look too human, so companies make different styles of robots.

In the future, robots will care for sick people and solve environmental problems. They will also help in disasters and make workplaces safer. Many people will have positive opinions about robots.

However, there will still be people who don't like robots. These people fear that we will rely on robots too much and we will lose important skills. Other people feel uncomfortable around robots.

Scientists will have to think about these different opinions so that when they make new robots, people will want to use them.

Summarize

Use details from the text to summarize the positive and negative effects of robots. Your graphic organizer may help you.

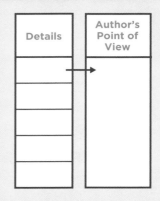

Text Evidence

1. How do you know that *What About Robots?* is an expository text? **GENRE**

2. What is the author's point of view in Chapter 3? What details from the text support this? **AUTHOR'S POINT OF VIEW**

3. The Greek prefix *auto-* means "self" or "same." Using this and context clues, figure out the meaning of *automatically* on page 4. Then find another word in the text that has this prefix and explain its meaning. **GREEK AND LATIN PREFIXES**

4. Write about the author's position on robots. Use details from the text in your answer. **WRITE ABOUT READING**

Compare Texts
Read an argument against using robots.

No Substitute

Some people say that in the future, every home will have a robot. Many people think this will be wonderful. Busy people will have more time and their lives will be better. In this essay, I hope to persuade you that a robot in every home would be a terrible thing.

People who have a machine to do their chores will become lazy. Children who don't do chores might not learn the value of hard work. Humans might stop taking responsibility for their actions.

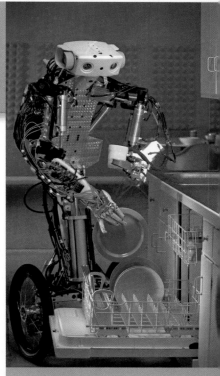

This robot was designed to help around the house.

19

Several companies have developed child-care robots. But parents or caregivers have a responsibility to raise children. They must teach their children how to behave. A robot cannot do this because robots can't feel emotions. They can't show kindness, sympathy, or love. Children raised by robots might not fully develop their emotions.

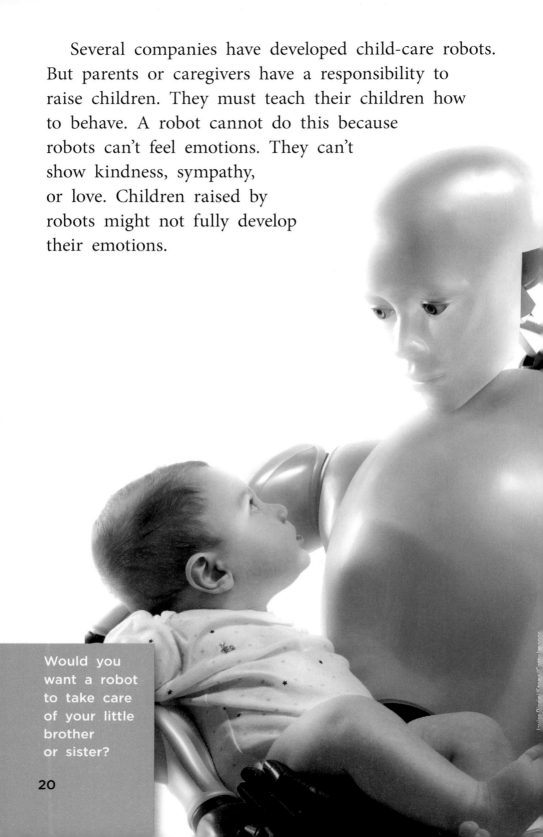

Would you want a robot to take care of your little brother or sister?

There are safety issues too. Robots can only do what they are programmed to do. In an emergency, a robot might not respond if it were not programmed to deal with the problem. This could be dangerous.

What if something unexpected went wrong while a robot was in charge? Would it be the fault of the robot, the robot's programmer, the robot's user, or the robot's owner?

What would happen to all the human workers the robots would replace? Workers including house cleaners, babysitters, and nurse companions could lose their jobs.

For all of these reasons, it is clear that a robot in every home is not a good idea.

Make Connections

What does *No Substitute* identify as the negative effects of using robots? ESSENTIAL QUESTION

After reading both texts, what is your point of view about robots? TEXT TO TEXT

Glossary

artificial *(ahr-tuh-FISH-uhl)* not natural; made by humans *(page 7)*

automatons *(aw-TOM-uh-tonz)* machines that follow a specific set of instructions; some look like humans or animals *(page 6)*

defuse *(dee-FYEWZ)* remove the fuse from a bomb so that it can't explode *(page 10)*

electronics *(i-lek-TRON-iks)* electrical circuits, devices, and equipment *(page 8)*

manufactured *(man-yuh-FAK-chuhrd)* made *(page 9)*

pollutants *(puh-LEW-tuhnts)* things that can harm the environment *(page 15)*

resources *(REE-sawrs-iz)* things that are useful to humans; for example, water, fuel, sunlight, forests, and food *(page 14)*

robotics *(roh-BOT-iks)* the branch of technology that deals with how robots are designed, built, and used *(page 3)*

sensors *(SEN-suhrz)* devices that can detect things, such as movement or light *(page 6)*

Index

Focus on Science

Purpose To explore what robots can and cannot do

Procedure

Step 1 ▶ Use the Internet to learn more about what robots can and cannot do.

Step 2 ▶ Make a two-column chart labeled "Can" and "Cannot." Record information about what robots can do and cannot do on your chart.

Step 3 ▶ Now make a chart for humans and record what humans can and cannot do.

Step 4 ▶ What is your opinion about robots versus humans? Use information from your charts to create a poster or a skit that compares robots with humans. Make sure you clearly show your point of view.

Conclusion Do you think the use of robots will become more common, less common, or stay the same as it is now? Why?